100 AMAZING FACTS ABOUT THE VIKINGS

© 2023, Marc Dresgui

Content

Introduction 8

Fact 1 - Viking soup: the meal of champions! 9

Fact 2 - Jewelry brooches... not just pretty! 10

Fact 3 - Wooden houses without nails or screws. 11

Fact 4 - Playing chess: a Viking sport? 12

Fact 5 - From warriors to helmets... without horns! 13

Fact 6 - The battle where they besieged Paris. 14

Fact 7 - Conquering America before Columbus! 15

Fact 8 - Stars as Viking GPS. 16

Fact 9 - Drakkar: the Viking dragon ship. 17

Fact 10 - Make a boat in a month? Possible! 18

Fact 11 - A compass... driftwood? 19

Fact 12 - Ships for trade and combat. 20

Fact 13 - Odin: the one-eyed god. 21

Fact 14 - Thor and his thunder hammer. 22

Fact 15 - Legends of rainbows and treasures. 23

Fact 16 - The Valkyries: Celestial Warriors 24

Fact 17 - The art of money: dazzling jewelry 25

Fact 18 - Mysterious messages engraved on stone 26

Fact 19 - Buried treasures to please the gods. 27

Fact 20 - The runes: the secret alphabet of the Vikings. ... 28

Fact 21 - The parties where everyone was dancing! 29

Fact 22 - Viking Mom: stronger than you think 30

Fact 23 - A wedding with swords and jewelry.................................31

Fact 24 - Funeral with boats and fires. 32

Fact 25 - Unexpected encounters with the English. 33

Fact 26 - Haggling with Byzantium: far from home.......................34

Fact 27 - Viking ambassadors among the Franks. 35

Fact 28 - Merging cultures: Vikings and Slavs................................36

Fact 29 - The warrior... Buried with a woman? 37

Fact 30 - Ragnar Lothbrok: myth or reality?...................................38

Fact 31 - The Viking princess in the East. 39

Fact 32 - Why they stopped their raids. 40

Fact 33 - Their descendants? Maybe your neighbor! 41

Fact 34 - The Normans: Vikings in France. 42

Fact 35 - The drakkars at war: naval power. 43

Fact 36 - The Saga of a Woman Explorer..44

Fact 37 - Decoding Viking symbols..45

Fact 38 - Raids: looting or trade?..46

Fact 39 - Eating sushi... Viking-style!..47

Fact 40 - The Northern Lights: sign of the gods.............................48

Fact 41 - Crossing Europe: the Viking journey. 49

Fact 42 - Skis to travel... and have fun. 50

Fact 43 - Fighting with round shields. 51

Fact 44 - The charm of Freyja's jewelry. 52

Fact 45 - Mead: the nectar of warriors..53

Fact 46 - Melodies played on lyres. 54

Fact 47 - The famous sagas written late. 55

Fact 48 - The riddle of the runestones. 56

Fact 49 - A board game for strategists. 57

Fact 50 - Goddess Loki: cunning and mischievous. 58

Fact 51 - Distant spices in the kitchen. 59

Fact 52 - The Battle of Stamford Bridge. 60

Fact 53 - Swords named and cherished. 61

Fact 54 - Viking tattoos: art and beliefs. 62

Fact 55 - The precious comb of every day. 63

Fact 56 - The mythical sea serpent. 64

Fact 57 - Hedeby's bustling market. 65

Fact 58 - The art of runes on bone and wood. 66

Fact 59 - Drakkars as graves. 67

Fact 60 - The truth about horned helmets. 68

Fact 61 - The mystery of the island of Greenland. 69

Fact 62 - The winter solstice festival. 70

Fact 63 - Circular forts: unique architecture. 71

Fact 64 - Viking knitting. 72

Fact 65 - Rare spices in their dishes. 73

Fact 66 - From Iceland to Newfoundland. 74

Fact 67 - Alliances with distant kings. 75

Fact 68 - The place of children in the sagas. 76

Fact 69 - The key role of women in business. 77

Fact 70 - The Jomsviking: elite warriors. 78

Fact 71 - The creation of the world according to them. 79

Fact 72 - The mysterious island named Vinland. 80

Fact 73 - The first map of the Viking world. 81

Fact 74 - The forgotten fortress of Danevirke. 82

Fact 75 - Sacred respect for nature. 83

Fact 76 - The legend of the berserkers. 84

Fact 77 - Write history with runes. 85

Fact 78 - The real treasure: talented slaves. 86

Fact 79 - Rival peoples and friends. 87

Fact 80 - The great Viking markets. 88

Fact 81 - The transition from paganism to Christianity. 89

Fact 82 - Jewelry to seduce and show its wealth. 90

Fact 83 - The first parliaments in Iceland. 91

Fact 84 - The gods of animals: wolf, raven. 92

Fact 85 - Feasts in honor of the gods. 93

Fact 86 - The mysterious red woman of Oseberg. 94

Fact 87 - How to educate a young Viking. 95

Fact 88 - Dancing and singing in the light of fire. 96

Fact 89 - The mystical sun compass. 97

Fact 90 - The sagas: stories of heroes and gods. 98

Fact 91 - The secret role of volvas (prophetesses). 99

Fact 92 - Raising eagles to hunt. 100

Fact 93 - Sailing with wind and currents. 101

Fact 94 - The rite of passage of the young warrior. 102

Fact 95 - The Faroese: Vikings of the islands. 103

Fact 96 - Teeth engraved to impress. 104

Fact 97 - Laws written on wood. 105

Fact 98 - Honoring a king with a ship-grave. 106

Fact 99 - The Vikings in Russia: elite merchants. 107

Fact 100 - Iceland's last Viking chieftain. 108

Conclusion 109

Quiz 110

Answers 116

"Better to leave the house and be a wanderer than to stay at home and lament all day."

— The Saga of Grettir

Introduction

History has always been populated by warriors, kings, explorers and artists who have shaped the course of humanity. Among them, the Vikings occupy a special place. These intrepid navigators, who came from the icy lands of the North, not only terrorized but also enriched Europe with their trade, culture and insatiable thirst for discovery. But who were really these men and women in horned helmets, whose sagas have survived the ages?

In "100 Amazing Facts About the Vikings", we unveil the life, myths and conquests of this fascinating people. From the mysterious tomb ship to berserker warriors, powerful prophetesses and bustling markets, this book takes you on a journey through a thousand years of history and legend. You'll discover stories that have shaped the world, amazing facts, and maybe some surprises.

Get ready, dear reader, to dive into the world of the Vikings, to feel the thrill of battles, the melody of skaldic poems and the wisdom of the ancients. Welcome to the adventure of the Viking world.

Marc Dresgui

Fact 1 - Viking soup: the meal of champions!

You probably wonder what the Vikings ate to have so much energy during their great expeditions. Well, the answer is simple: soup! Yes, you read that right. These fearsome warriors of the North loved good old soup.

In general, they used local ingredients, such as fish or meat, that they had hunted or caught themselves. They added vegetables, herbs and sometimes even grains. It was a nourishing meal that gave the Vikings all the nutrients they needed for their long days.

This soup was cooked in large iron cauldrons, suspended over a fire. The whole village gathered around the fire, sharing stories and laughter as the soup simmered. It was a real moment of conviviality.

So next time you eat soup, think about the Vikings and their incredible adventures. Maybe this simple soup will give you, too, the strength of a Viking warrior!

Fact 2 - Jewelry brooches... not just pretty!

You've seen braces before, haven't you? These little jewels that we hang on our clothes to decorate them. Among the Vikings, these pins had a double function: they were both aesthetic and practical!

These brooches, often called "fibulae", were essential for Viking women. They were used to hold their dresses or coats in place. Made of metal, bone, or even ivory, these fibulas were often decorated with intricate patterns, such as interlacing, animals, or mythological figures.

But that wasn't all! These jewels also had social significance. The patterns, materials used, and the size of the pins could indicate the social status of the person wearing them. A brooch rich in detail, for example, was probably worn by a woman of high society.

The next time you wear a brooch or a pin, think about those Vikings and the rich history behind such a small object. Who knows, maybe your jewel will make you look like a Viking warrior!

Fact 3 - Wooden houses without nails or screws.

Imagine building a house without using nails or screws! Sounds impossible, doesn't it? Yet that's exactly what the Vikings did. Unbelievable, don't you think?

The Vikings were true masters of wood. They used a technique called "tenon and mortise framing". Basically, it means that they fit the pieces of wood into each other, much like you would with building bricks. These assemblies were then held in place with wooden dowels.

Their method was so solid that many Viking houses and buildings survived for centuries! These constructions were often covered with a thick layer of peat to insulate them from the cold and wind.

So the next time you find yourself facing a puzzle or a construction game, remember the Vikings and their amazing wooden houses. With a little ingenuity and patience, you can create wonders, just like them!

Fact 4 - Playing chess: a Viking sport?

When you think of the Vikings, you probably imagine warriors in battle, don't you? Well, prepare to be surprised: these same warriors also loved to play... to chess!

Yes, that's right. Chess, the strategic game we know well today, was also popular among the Vikings. They had their own version, called "hnefatafl", but the principles were similar: two players, pieces to move, and an objective to defeat the opposing king.

Beautifully carved bone and ivory chess pieces have been discovered during archaeological excavations at Viking sites. These pieces testify not only to their love for acting, but also to their remarkable artistic talent.

So next time you play chess, think about those Vikings strategists. By moving your pawns and planning your attacks, you may walk in the footsteps of these fearsome players from the North!

Fact 5 - From warriors to helmets... without horns!

When we talk to you about the Vikings, you probably imagine warriors wearing heavy helmets adorned with large horns. Think again, it's actually a myth!

Yes, despite what the movies and cartoons show, the Vikings did not wear horned helmets during battles. It is a relatively recent invention of popular culture. In reality, these helmets would even be very impractical in combat: the horns could easily get stuck or be grabbed by an opponent.

True Viking helmets were rather simple, usually made of metal, and had the main purpose of protecting the head from blows. Some were equipped with a nasal protection, but this was the only "decoration" they featured.

So the next time you see a picture of a Viking with a horned helmet, you can smile knowing the truth. And who knows, you might even impress your friends by telling them this surprising fact about the real warriors of the North!

Fact 6 - The battle where they besieged Paris.

You know Paris, this magnificent city of light, don't you? Well, imagine it, in the year 845, surrounded by a horde of 5,000 Vikings! That is exactly what happened.

Led by a feared leader named Ragnar Lodbrok, these warriors from the North sailed the Seine with a fleet of 120 ships. Their goal? Plunder the rich city of Paris. Parisians, though terrified, valiantly defended themselves.

Despite the resistance of the city, the Vikings finally managed to enter and loot it. In exchange for their departure, King Charles the Bald had to pay them a huge ransom. It was a significant episode in the history of interactions between the Vikings and the Frankish kingdom.

So, the next time you walk the streets of Paris, think about that distant time when intrepid Viking warriors walked those same cobblestones. History is really all around us, isn't it?

Fact 7 - Conquering America before Columbus!

Have you ever heard that Christopher Columbus was the first European to discover America? Well, think again! The Vikings preceded it by almost 500 years!

It was around the year 1000 that Leif Erikson, a Viking explorer, is said to have reached the shores of what we now call Canada. He named this land "Vinland", because of the wild vines he found there. Fascinating, isn't it?

The most famous site associated with this Viking expedition to America is L'Anse aux Meadows, located in Newfoundland. Archaeologists have discovered the remains of Viking houses and tools, irrefutable proof of their presence.

Just imagine: Vikings sailing through the frigid waters of the North Atlantic, arriving on a mysterious new continent. Thanks to them, the story of America's discovery takes a completely different turn. Impressive, isn't it?

Fact 8 - Stars as Viking GPS.

You probably use an app or GPS to find your way around on the go. But do you know how the Vikings did without these modern technologies? They were turning to the sky!

Indeed, these exceptional navigators used the stars to orient themselves at sea. The North Star, in particular, was of great help as it always points north. By observing its position, the Vikings could determine their direction with astonishing accuracy.

But it wasn't their only tool. They also used "solar stones", crystals that, when oriented towards the sun, made it possible to determine its position even on overcast days. Amazing, isn't it?

Thanks to their great knowledge of the sky and a few ingenious tricks, the Vikings were able to explore distant territories, long before the era of modern technology. The next time you look up at the stars, remember the Vikings and their incredible journeys guided by the twinkling night sky.

Fact 9 - Drakkar: the Viking dragon ship.

You've probably seen those long boats with a strange figurehead that looks like a dragon, haven't you? These are the drakkars, the famous Viking ships!

These boats were fast, light and extremely maneuverable. Thanks to their shallow draft, they could sail on the high seas as well as on shallow rivers, which was ideal for surprising their enemies or exploring new territories.

The dragon-shaped figurehead was not just an ornament. It served to frighten enemies and protect the crew from evil spirits. It was also a sign of power and status for the Viking leader who owned the ship.

So the next time you see a drakkar, whether in a museum or in a movie, remember that it's not just a boat, but a powerful symbol of the Viking Age. A true masterpiece of marine engineering of the time!

Fact 10 - Make a boat in a month? Possible!

Imagine you want to build a boat. How long do you think it would take? One year? Several months? Well, for the Vikings, it was a matter of weeks!

Using simple tools and incredible carpentry skills, the Vikings could assemble a ship in as little as a month. Unbelievable, right? They mainly used oak wood, known for its robustness, to build the hull of the boat.

Their technique was based on "clinching", a process where wooden planks were superimposed and fixed together by iron rivets. This gave the boat a solid structure while making it lightweight and flexible, perfect for rushing waters.

So, if you're wondering how the Vikings managed to explore so many territories and become such fearsome warriors at sea, part of the answer lies in their incredible ability to quickly build efficient boats. Isn't it fascinating how advanced they were in the art of shipbuilding?

Fact 11 - A compass... driftwood?

You probably use a modern metal or plastic compass to find your way around. But do you know what material the Vikings used for their compasses? Driftwood!

Yes, you heard right! These ingenious navigators used lightweight, water-resistant pieces of driftwood as the basis for their compasses. But how did it work?

Using an iron rod that they "magnetized" by rubbing it with a magnetic stone (magnetite), they then placed it on a piece of driftwood. This rod, free to move, then pointed north, helping the Vikings to orient themselves.

This simple but effective navigational instrument shows how innovative the Vikings were. Using the resources at their disposal and applying their knowledge, they have created a valuable tool for their maritime expeditions.

So the next time you have a compass in your hands, remember the Vikings and their clever use of driftwood to orient themselves on the vast oceans. Impressive, isn't it?

Fact 12 - Ships for trade and combat.

You probably think the Vikings only used their boats for raids and fighting, right? Think again! These astute navigators had different types of ships for different needs.

The famous "drakkars", which you may have already seen with their imposing dragon-shaped figureheads, were mainly used for wars. Fast and agile, they were perfect for surprising enemies.

But the Vikings also had "knarrs", ships designed specifically for trade. Larger and with a larger cargo capacity, they were optimized to transport goods, such as furs, timber, and even slaves, across the seas.

This shows how skilled the Vikings were and not just warriors. Their ability to build different types of vessels for various activities demonstrates their ingenuity and adaptability.

So, the next time you hear about the Vikings, don't forget that they were also excellent merchants, as well as daring warriors of the seas!

Fact 13 - Odin: the one-eyed god.

You've probably heard of Greek or Roman gods. But do you know the Norse gods, dear to the Vikings? One of the most powerful and mysterious is Odin, the one-eyed god!

Odin is often depicted as an old bearded man with a stick, riding an eight-legged horse named Sleipnir. But why does he have only one eye, you ask? That's a fascinating story!

To gain wisdom and knowledge, Odin sacrificed his eye by throwing it into the spring of Mímir. In exchange, he could drink water from this spring, giving him an unprecedented vision and understanding of the worlds.

This sacrifice shows how important the quest for knowledge was to Odin and to Viking culture in general. They valued wisdom as much as strength in battle.

Thus, throughout the story of Odin, the Vikings remind us of the importance of knowledge, and sometimes, the sacrifices that must be made to obtain it. Always a relevant lesson, isn't it?

Fact 14 - Thor and his thunder hammer.

If I tell you about Thor, you might think of the superhero with his shiny suit and giant hammer. But did you know that the original Thor is a Viking god, son of Odin, and has a very special hammer?

This hammer, called Mjölnir, was not only a formidable weapon. It symbolized the protection of the gods towards humans. Every time Thor threw it, it produced thunder, and after hitting its target, the hammer always came back to him.

But this hammer was not easy to wield. Only Thor, thanks to his immense strength and magic gloves, could lift and throw him. This detail shows how powerful Thor was considered among gods and mortals.

So the next time you see Thor in a movie or comic book, remember his Viking origins and the importance of his thunderhammer. It is much more than just a weapon, it is a symbol of protection and power!

Fact 15 - Legends of rainbows and treasures.

Have you ever dreamed of finding the treasure hidden at the end of a rainbow? For the Vikings, this idea was not so far from their mythology! Want to know more? Fasten your seatbelt and get ready for a colorful journey.

The rainbow, for the Vikings, was not just a weather phenomenon. It was the Bifröst, a magical bridge connecting the world of humans, Midgard, to the world of the gods, Asgard. Just imagine: walking on colors to meet the gods!

But be careful! This bridge was guarded by Heimdall, the divine guardian with ultra-sophisticated sight and hearing. He made sure that the giants, enemies of the gods, did not use it to invade Asgard.

And the treasure in all this? Well, the most precious treasure for the Vikings was not gold or precious stones. It was the wisdom, stories and lessons of their myths. And with this legend, they remind us that beauty and magic can hide where we least expect it. Magical, isn't it?

Fact 16 - The Valkyries: Celestial Warriors.

Have you ever heard of winged warriors flying over battlefields? No, this is not a fantasy film, but a part of Viking mythology! I introduce you to the Valkyries, fascinating figures of Nordic culture.

These powerful women, often depicted with wings, had a very specific role in combat. They chose the most valiant warriors fallen in battle to take them to Valhalla, the great hall of Odin, where they prepared for the final battle, the Ragnarök.

But that wasn't all! The Valkyries didn't just serve as escorts for heroes. In Valhalla, they also served as hostesses, preparing feasts and filling the horns with mead for the brave who were welcomed there.

So if you hear about flying warriors, battle angels, or heavenly messengers in other cultures, think of the Valkyries. These legendary figures show us that the Vikings had a great admiration for courage, sacrifice and honor in battle.

Fact 17 - The art of money: dazzling jewelry.

Have you ever admired a piece of jewelry and wondered how it was made? Just imagine: the Vikings, without the modern tools, managed to create real masterpieces in silver!

Silver was very valuable to the Vikings, and they used it to make beautiful jewelry. Necklaces, bracelets, rings and brooches, these objects often reflected the wealth and status of the wearer. But it wasn't just for appearance!

In addition to being aesthetic, these jewels also had practical value. They could be dismantled or cut into pieces to serve as currency in trade. It's clever, right?

But beyond their function, the art of Viking money testifies to their exceptional know-how. The intricate patterns, interlacing and stylized animals engraved on these jewels show just how gifted the Vikings were. So, the next time you wear a piece of jewelry, think about the history and culture it might hide!

Fact 18 - Mysterious messages engraved on stone.

Imagine walking in nature and falling on a huge stone covered with strange symbols. This is exactly what is found in parts of Scandinavia: Viking runestones!

The Vikings used an ancient alphabet called runes to write. These symbols were often engraved on large stones to commemorate important events, fallen heroes or to mark territories.

But what's really intriguing is the mystery surrounding some of these inscriptions. Despite the best efforts of historians, some runestones carry messages that remain enigmatic. Maybe forgotten legends or love stories?

These stones are also a window into the past. They show us the beliefs, aspirations and daily life of the Vikings. Each inscription tells a story, a piece of a bygone era.

The next time you write a message, imagine yourself carving every word in stone for future generations to read. What story would you like to tell them?

Fact 19 - Buried treasures to please the gods.

Just imagine: you're walking in a field, and suddenly you're tripping over something metallic. By digging, you discover a Viking treasure! Sound crazy? Still, it really happened!

The Vikings used to bury valuables in the earth. What for? To offer sacrifices to their gods. It was their way of showing their devotion and hoping for favors in return. Gold, silver, jewelry... They were burying real fortunes!

Sometimes they hid these treasures in times of war, hoping to recover them later. But often, they never returned, leaving these riches to wait centuries underground.

Thanks to these discoveries, much is known about Viking craftsmanship and what they considered valuable. And you, what would you offer to the gods if you wanted to win their favor? One thing is certain: these Vikings really knew how to impress!

Fact 20 - The runes: the secret alphabet of the Vikings.

Have you ever seen strange symbols engraved on stones or jewelry? These mysterious inscriptions are runes, the secret writing of the Vikings! Not only did they write with it, but these symbols also had magical powers.

Each rune has a special meaning. For example, "Raido" looks like the letter "R" and means "journey". By engraving this rune on an object, the Vikings believed that they would be protected during their distant adventures.

Runes were not only used for writing. They were also used in rituals. Priests and soothsayers threw them, much like dice, to predict the future or make important decisions.

So the next time you see these enigmatic symbols, remember that they are much more than just letters. They are a gateway to the mystery and magic of the Viking Age. And you, if you had your own runic symbol, what would it be?

Fact 21 - The parties where everyone was dancing!

Can you imagine a great Viking dancing happily around a fire? This is exactly what happened during the great Viking festivals! These festivities were times to celebrate, relax and, of course, dance.

These festivals were often held to mark important events, such as the end of the harvest or the arrival of the winter solstice. Everyone gathered from warriors to farmers, and even children took part in the dance.

Music was played with instruments such as lutes, drums and flutes. Under the stars, the Vikings whirled, jumped and sang in rhythm, creating an electric atmosphere.

So the next time you dance and let yourself be carried away by the music, remember that even the fearsome Vikings knew how to have fun and celebrate life with enthusiasm. And you, would you be ready to dance the Viking way?

Fact 22 - Viking Mom: stronger than you think.

Did you know that Viking moms weren't just housewives? Oh no, they were much more than that. While their men went on expeditions, these women took over the management of the house, the land and even the trade.

That was not all. In Viking society, women enjoyed significant rights. They could own land, divorce their husbands if necessary, and be respected chiefs within their communities.

But their role was not limited to domestic affairs. Some Viking women, called "shieldmaidens", even entered the battlefield, ready to defend their homes and families. Sagas and ancient texts speak of these warriors who fought with as much courage and strength as their male counterparts.

So the next time you think of a Viking mother, don't just imagine a housewife. Instead, visualize a leader, a warrior, a force of nature that played a crucial role in rich Viking history.

Fact 23 - A wedding with swords and jewelry.

You're probably wondering what a wedding was like in the Viking Age, aren't you? Well, know that it was a ceremony rich in symbols and traditions, very different from what you could imagine.

First, swords had a place of honor during these unions. The groom-to-be offered an ancestral sword to his bride, symbolizing protection and strength. For her part, the bride gave her husband her childhood sword, marking the transition from her parental protection to that of her husband.

But jewelry also played a key role. Brides often wore silver necklaces and bracelets, reflecting their dowry and social status. These jewels, passed down from generation to generation, were as much pieces of art as markers of wealth.

Finally, the ceremony usually ended with a large banquet, where all the guests celebrated the new union. Songs, dances and feasts punctuated this memorable day, sealing the love and complicity of the newlyweds.

Fact 24 - Funeral with boats and fires.

Have you ever heard of the spectacular Viking funeral? Far from being a simple ceremony, these funeral rites reflected the importance of the deceased and his place in Viking society.

The Vikings believed in an afterlife and, to ensure that the deceased was well prepared for this new adventure, they organized a grandiose funeral. For the most prestigious, a boat was often used as a grave. The body was placed on board, surrounded by its possessions, weapons, food and sometimes even sacrificed servants.

But that was not all. These boats were often set on fire. Fire, in the eyes of the Vikings, purified and allowed the soul of the deceased to rise to Valhalla, the mythical room where fallen warriors joined the god Odin.

These rites, impressive and loaded with symbolism, show how life, death and spirituality were intimately linked in Viking culture. A poetic and powerful way to say goodbye to their loved ones, while celebrating their passage to the afterlife.

Fact 25 - Unexpected encounters with the English.

Did you know that the Vikings were not only invaders for the English? Their encounters, far from always confrontational, have shaped the history of the British Isles in an astonishing way.

As early as the end of the 8th century, the Vikings began their raids on the English coast. However, over time, these raids turned into real installations. The Vikings established settlements, gradually mixing with the local population. This cohabitation has given rise to intense cultural and commercial exchanges.

Many English cities, such as York, have Viking origins. The English words "skirt" and "knife" are also of Norse origin. The Vikings left an indelible mark on the English language and culture.

These interactions between Vikings and English show that history is never simple. Relations between peoples can evolve from confrontation to collaboration. And it is this mixture and this exchange that make the richness of our past.

Fact 26 - Haggling with Byzantium: far from home.

You think of the Vikings as tough warriors of the North, don't you? But did you know that they were also skilled traders who established trade routes as far as Byzantium, present-day Istanbul?

The Viking world was vast and their thirst for adventure drove them to sail away from their Scandinavian homes. In search of valuable goods, they followed Russian rivers, forging trade links with the mighty Byzantine Empire. There they exchanged their Nordic possessions for luxurious fabrics, spices and other riches.

It was not uncommon for some Vikings to settle and serve as mercenaries in the Varangian Guard, the elite of the Byzantine armed forces. These warriors, mainly from Sweden, were highly respected for their bravery in battle.

These cultural and commercial exchanges show another facet of the Vikings, far from the cliché of bloodthirsty looters. Their ability to integrate and trade with such distant civilizations is a testament to their adaptability and open-mindedness.

Fact 27 - Viking ambassadors among the Franks.

You may imagine the Vikings as fierce conquerors, but do you know that they have not always been at war with the people they have encountered? In fact, they even sent ambassadors to establish diplomatic relations, notably with the Frankish Empire.

In the ninth century, when the Vikings raided Frankish territory, these interactions were not limited to combat. Viking leaders, recognizing the strategic importance of the Carolingian Empire, sought alliances and peace agreements. To do this, they sent ambassadors to the Francian court.

These envoys were tasked with negotiating treaties, creating matrimonial alliances, and securing territories. One of the most notable consequences of these talks was the Treaty of Saint-Clair-sur-Epte in 911, which granted the Vikings Normandy in exchange for protection from further invaders.

Thus, far from the image of brutal invaders, the Vikings were also shrewd strategists and diplomats, able to negotiate skillfully with the great powers of their time.

Fact 28 - Merging cultures: Vikings and Slavs.

When we talk about the Vikings, we often think of their raids in Western Europe. But do you know that they also played a crucial role in the east, interacting deeply with the Slavs? This cultural mix has left a lasting imprint on history.

Vikings, mainly from Scandinavia, sailed along Russia's major rivers, such as the Volga and Dnieper. In the course of their travels, they established trading posts and mingled with the local Slavic populations. These interactions have led to not only commercial, but also cultural exchanges.

The fusion of the Vikings and Slavs resulted in the formation of the state of Kievan Rus', the forerunner of modern Russia. The very name "Rus" is of Scandinavian origin, probably related to the word "rods-", meaning "rowing". Viking rulers, called Varangians, were instrumental in establishing this state.

Thus, by mixing trade, exploration and diplomacy, Vikings and Slavs forged ties that shaped much of Eastern European history. A beautiful lesson on how two cultures can come together and create something bigger together.

Fact 29 - The warrior... Buried with a woman?

Surely you have heard of the fearsome Viking warriors, with their sharp weapons and impressive armor. But did you know that sometimes the graves of these warriors reveal unexpected surprises?

In the town of Birka, Sweden, a tomb dating back to the 10th century has been discovered. It contained a set of weapons typical of a warrior, such as a sword, axe and arrows. At first glance, nothing fancy. However, DNA analysis revealed that the skeleton belonged to a woman!

This discovery has shaken up some preconceived ideas about Viking society. She demonstrated that women could also hold fighting positions and be buried with the honors reserved for warriors. It reminds us how essential it is to move away from stereotypes and to deepen our understanding of ancient cultures.

So the next time you imagine a Viking warrior, don't forget that he might as well be a warrior! A reminder that the past can always hold surprises.

Fact 30 - Ragnar Lothbrok: myth or reality?

You may have heard of Ragnar Lothbrok, the famous Viking king, thanks to TV series and epic tales. But do you wonder if this legendary man really existed?

The Norse sagas, these ancient Scandinavian stories, portray Ragnar as an extraordinary hero, accomplishing incredible feats, from fighting a giant snake to his daring raids on Paris. Are these stories, although enriched with fantastic elements, pure fiction or are they rooted in reality?

Historians are divided. Some believe that Ragnar was an amalgam of several historical figures, while others believe that he may have been an actual Viking leader, exaggerated by oral tradition over time. What is certain is that there is no concrete evidence of its existence.

Whether he was a real man or a myth, Ragnar Lothbrok's influence in popular culture is undeniable. His name evokes the golden age of the Vikings, and his legacy continues to inspire and fascinate.

Fact 31 - The Viking princess in the East.

Have you ever heard of a Viking princess who finds herself in the East? This story, as fascinating as it is unusual, reminds us of the extent of the Vikings' travels.

During the golden age of the Vikings, their expeditions were not limited to Europe. Driven by trade and adventure, some sailed to lands as far away as Byzantium, present-day Istanbul. At the heart of this period, a Scandinavian princess, according to legends, would have made such a trip.

The details of her trip are unclear, but chronicles suggest she may have been a merchant or even an ambassador. Its presence in the East testifies to the cultural and commercial interactions between the Vikings and the Byzantine world.

The truth behind this princess remains mysterious. Nevertheless, its history illustrates the impressive reach of the Vikings and their ability to integrate into diverse cultures, even thousands of miles from their northern homeland.

Fact 32 - Why they stopped their raids.

Viking raids have become legendary. For centuries, their expeditions have spread terror on European shores. But have you ever wondered why these raids suddenly stopped?

First, the gradual conversion to Christianity played a major role. By embracing this new faith, the Vikings adopted a worldview less focused on conquest and plunder. Christianity provided a moral framework that curbed these incursions.

Moreover, political structures in Europe have evolved. Kingdoms grew stronger, and stronger coastal defenses were put in place, making raids less successful and riskier for the Vikings.

Finally, economic integration has also played a role. The Vikings began to establish settlements and trade peacefully rather than plunder. This transition to established trade relationships offered more lasting benefits than raids.

Thus, between faith, politics and economy, the Vikings gradually abandoned their former life as raiders to anchor themselves in a changing Europe.

Fact 33 - Their descendants? Maybe your neighbor!

The Vikings, those navigators and warriors of the North, did not simply disappear. In fact, you'd be surprised to learn how many people today share Viking ancestry.

For centuries, the Vikings established settlements and mingled with local populations in many areas, from Russia to Iceland, France to Britain. Each time they settled, they left an indelible genetic mark in these populations.

Recent genetic studies have revealed that many Europeans have Viking ancestry. If you live in northern Europe or if your family comes from there, chances are you carry with you a part of this northern heritage.

So the next time you run into someone on the street or chat with your neighbor, remember: their great-great-great-grandfather or grandmother could very well have been a Viking! The legacy of these daring explorers lives on, in the veins of millions of us.

Fact 34 - The Normans: Vikings in France.

The Vikings, you can probably imagine them plundering and sailing the North Seas. But did you know that some of them eventually settled in France? They became what we call today the "Normans".

In the ninth century, these Vikings began to conduct raids on the French coast. Attracted by the wealth of the territory, they decided to settle there. In 911, the Treaty of Saint-Clair-sur-Epte was signed between the King of the Franks, Charles the Simple, and the Viking leader Rollo. In exchange for the kingdom's protection from further Viking raids, Rollo received part of the region, which would become Normandy.

Over the years, these Vikings assimilated into the local culture. They adopted the French language, religion and customs. Thus, in a few generations, these warriors of the North became powerful dukes and cathedral builders.

So the next time you hear about the Normans or Normandy, remember their Viking roots and the indelible mark they left on French history.

Fact 35 - The drakkars at war: naval power.

You have probably already heard of the drakkars, these imposing boats with the bow adorned with a dragon's head. But do you really know how essential these ships were in the warrior power of the Vikings?

These boats were designed to be fast and maneuverable. Their flat bottoms allowed them to sail on both the high seas and shallow waters, giving them an undeniable tactical advantage. They could access the rivers, surprise their enemies and leave before anyone could react.

The effectiveness of the drakkar was not limited to its speed. Its sturdy construction and ability to carry large numbers of warriors made it a formidable war machine. The Vikings could land quickly, plunder and return to sea in a flash.

Thus, thanks to their drakkars, the Vikings not only dominated the North Seas, but also extended their influence far beyond their homelands. A true demonstration of the naval power of the time!

Fact 36 - The Saga of a Woman Explorer.

Did you know that among the Vikings, there were women who stood out as much as their male counterparts? Yes, that's right! One of them is Gudrid Thorbjarnardottir, a woman whose story is as fascinating as that of the greatest explorers.

Born in Iceland, Gudrid was not just a villager. According to the Icelandic sagas, she traveled through Greenland and as far as North America, long before Christopher Columbus. This makes her one of the first Europeans to set foot on the American continent.

But that's not all. She also helped found a Viking settlement in Vinland (now Newfoundland, Canada). The saga tells that she gave birth to a son, Snorri, who would be the first European child born in America.

Its history, engraved in the sagas, testifies to the audacity and bravery of Viking women. Gudrid is a shining example that, in the world of the Vikings, exploits were not reserved for men.

Fact 37 - Decoding Viking symbols.

Have you ever wondered what these mysterious symbols engraved on Viking jewelry, weapons and runestones represent? Let's dive into this captivating universe together to discover more.

The Vikings used a variety of symbols, each with a particular meaning. For example, the Valknut, represented by three intertwined triangles, is often associated with Odin, the supreme god, and death in battle. This symbol, seen on many objects, evoked divine power and the passage to the afterlife.

Another iconic symbol is the Aegishjalmur or "Helm of Awe". It is formed by eight radiating branches around a central circle. It was a symbol of protection and power, worn by warriors to protect them in battle.

Finally, the Yggdrasil, the tree of life that binds the nine worlds in Norse mythology, is frequently depicted. Symbolizing the interconnectedness of all things, it recalls the depth of Viking beliefs. Each symbol offers valuable insight into their world, beliefs, and view of the universe.

Fact 38 - Raids: looting or trade?

When you think of the Vikings, you probably imagine fierce warriors landing on the coast to plunder and destroy. Yet this image tells only part of the story.

Certainly, the Vikings were masters when it came to raiding. They used their swift and maneuverable drakkars to carry out surprise attacks, often targeting monasteries rich in treasures. This looting earned them a formidable reputation throughout Europe.

However, besides their raids, the Vikings were also skilled traders. They established trade routes stretching from Scandinavia to Asia, North Africa and even North America. They traded furs, amber, slaves, spices and many other goods.

Thus, if their raids made an impression, it is essential to remember that the Vikings were not only looters. Their ability to trade and interact with diverse cultures was instrumental in shaping the history of medieval Europe.

Fact 39 - Eating sushi... Viking-style!

You love sushi, don't you? Well, imagine that the Vikings had their own version of this delicacy. Far from the rice fields of Japan, the warriors of the North knew how to appreciate the taste of raw fish.

In Scandinavia, much of the Vikings' diet was based on the sea. They mastered the art of preserving fish by drying, smoking or salting it. But one of their favorite dishes was "gravlax," raw salmon marinated in a mixture of salt, sugar, and dill.

But wait, that wasn't all! The Vikings often accompanied their gravlax with dense black bread, fresh herbs and a mustard and herb sauce, a far cry from the soy sauce you use today for your sushi.

So even though Japanese sushi and Viking gravlax are different in their preparation, they share one thing in common: celebrating the pure, delicate taste of raw fish. Who would have thought you had a Viking palace?

Fact 40 - The Northern Lights: sign of the gods.

You've seen pictures of those shimmering lights in the night sky, haven't you? These Northern Lights, which enchant our eyes, were for the Vikings much more than just a celestial spectacle.

For these northern navigators, these glows were intimately linked to their cosmogony. Some believed that these lights were a reflection of the armor of the Valkyries, the celestial warriors who took the souls of fallen warriors to Valhalla, the great hall where heroes feasted with the gods.

Others thought it was Bifrost, the rainbow bridge connecting the world of men to that of the gods. This bridge, according to Norse mythology, was the route that the gods took to interact with mortals.

So the next time you see those beautiful dancing glows in the sky, remember how important they were to the Vikings. A visual spectacle, certainly, but also a profound reminder of the connection between man, nature and divinities.

Fact 41 - Crossing Europe: the Viking journey.

Have you ever imagined traveling all over Europe without GPS, detailed maps or even a reliable compass? For the Vikings, it was a reality. These intrepid navigators not only had the courage to venture on the high seas, they did so with astonishing precision.

From their Scandinavian homes, they sailed westward, reaching the British Isles, Ireland, and even Iceland, Greenland, and eventually North America. But they didn't just explore west. To the east, they crossed rivers such as the Volga, traded with Byzantium and even established colonies like that of Rus', the forerunner of modern Russia.

These trips were not always peaceful. They involved raids, businesses and sometimes permanent settlements. The Vikings left a lasting imprint on the territories they passed through, shaping the history of many regions.

So the next time you look at a map of Europe, think of those daring Vikings who, without modern technology, crossed entire continents, leaving their mark every step of the way.

Fact 42 - Skis to travel... and have fun.

When you think of skis, you probably imagine a holiday in the mountains and snowy descents. But did you know that the Vikings were already using skis more than a thousand years ago, and not just for fun?

In Scandinavia, where winters are long and snowy, skis were essential for getting around. They allowed the Vikings to travel great distances, hunt or even conduct winter raids. The first archaeological evidence of skis in Scandinavia dates back more than 5,000 years!

But these brave warriors were not only serious. Sagas, ancient texts, refer to ski competitions and games. Just imagine: Vikings hurtling down the slopes, competing in skill and speed, for glory and entertainment!

So the next time you put on your skis, remember that you're sharing a hobby with ancient Scandinavian navigators, warriors, and explorers. And maybe you're even continuing a tradition that goes back millennia.

Fact 43 - Fighting with round shields.

If you've ever wondered how the Vikings defend themselves in battle, look at their shields. These large wooden discs, often painted and ornate, were more than just accessories: they were an essential part of Viking strategy on the battlefield.

The round shield, usually about one meter in diameter, was designed to protect the warrior from enemy attacks. Light and maneuverable, it was used as much in defense as in attack. In tight formation, the shields overlapped, forming an almost impenetrable "wall".

But that was not all. The edges of these shields were sometimes reinforced with leather or metal, allowing the Vikings to strike or repel their opponents. The fighting was brutal, and every advantage was vital.

So the next time you see a round shield in a museum or Viking movie, remember its importance. It was not just a protection, but a weapon in its own right in the hands of a seasoned warrior.

Fact 44 - The charm of Freyja's jewelry.

Have you ever heard of the enchanting jewelry of Freyja, the Viking goddess of love and beauty? These mystical ornaments captured not only the eye but also the legends.

Freyja had a necklace named Brísingamen, of unparalleled beauty. According to Norse mythology, she obtained it after seducing the four dwarves who had forged it. This sparkling necklace symbolized her power and seduction.

But this jewel was not just an ornament. It was said that Brísingamen had magical powers. Some say that he bestowed on Freyja supernatural abilities, strengthening her position among the gods.

The next time you admire a sparkling jewel or necklace, remember the legendary charm of Brísingamen. Behind every gemstone, there could be a story as fascinating as that of Goddess Freyja and her precious treasure.

Fact 45 - Mead: the nectar of warriors.

Have you ever tasted mead, the golden drink that makes the eyes of Vikings sparkle at the mere mention of it? Mead, fermented from water, honey and yeast, has a history as rich as its taste.

In Viking times, this drink was considered the nectar of warriors. It was often eaten at feasts and celebrations, symbolizing bravery in battle and the strength of the Viking spirit. It was a drink of choice to honor gods and heroes.

Mead was not limited to its festive function. According to Norse mythology, it was also associated with poetry and inspiration. Odin himself, the supreme god, once stole the sacred mead to give to men, thus offering them the gift of poetry.

The next time you raise your glass, think of those ancient Norse warriors, celebrating their victories with the sweet scent of mead. A tradition, a symbol, a story with every sip.

Fact 46 - Melodies played on lyres.

Imagine yourself in the heart of a large Viking hall, lit by torches, where sweet and haunting melodies rise into the air. These sounds come from an instrument very popular at that time: the lyre.

The Viking lyre, usually with six to eight strings, was made from carefully carved wood and sometimes adorned with delicate inlays. It was played with the fingers or a plectrum, thus producing varied and harmonious melodies.

The melodies played on these lyres often accompanied poems and sagas, telling stories of heroes, love or gods. In this culture where oral art held a prominent place, the lyre became the perfect complement to enhance the magic of stories.

The next time you hear the sweet notes of a lyre, close your eyes. Let yourself be transported to those ancient times, when musicians and storytellers enchanted their audience with their combined talents. A time when music and history were one.

Fact 47 - The famous sagas written late.

When you think of the Vikings, you probably imagine fierce warriors, drakkars and... sagas. These epic oral stories, which have survived the ages, contain the very essence of Viking culture. But did you know that the majority of them were not written down until well after the Viking Age?

In reality, the sagas, despite their antiquity, were not recorded on parchment until the 13th century, mainly in Iceland. They were transmitted orally from generation to generation, transforming and evolving over time, before finally being recorded.

These detailed stories, rich in characters and intrigues, tell the life, travels, conflicts and passions of the northern peoples. Although they are written down late, they offer an invaluable insight into Viking society, beliefs and customs.

The next time you dive into a saga, remember that it is the fruit of a long oral tradition, shaped by countless voices, before being immortalized on paper centuries later.

Fact 48 - The riddle of the runestones.

While walking through the landscapes of the North, you could come across mysterious engraved stones: runestones. These monoliths, scattered mainly in Scandinavia, are silent witnesses of the Viking Age. But do you really know what they are hiding?

These stones, often erected in memory of a deceased loved one or to commemorate an event, are engraved with runes. It is an ancient alphabet used by the Germanic peoples. Each rune has not only a phonetic meaning, but also a symbolic one.

Yet, despite the efforts of researchers, some of these inscriptions remain enigmatic. They can hide stories, myths or incantations whose precise meaning has been lost over time. It also happens that stones are deliberately cryptic, perhaps to be understood only by an elite.

The next time you come across one of these granite sentinels, take a moment to think about the secrets it might hold. The runestones are not simple engravings, but portals to the mysterious past of the Vikings.

Fact 49 - A board game for strategists.

Have you ever wondered how the Vikings spend their free time when they're not raiding or exploring? One of their favorite distractions was a board game called Hnefatafl. This game, which means "king's table", was much more than just entertainment.

Hnefatafl is an asymmetrical game: one player commands the king and his defenders while the other leads the attackers. The goal? For the king, reach one of the edges of the plateau. For the attackers, capture him. Strategy is crucial, much like chess.

Pieces of this game have been found during archaeological excavations throughout Scandinavia, proving its cultural significance. It was not only played for fun, but also to train minds in tactics and strategy, essential skills for a people often in conflict.

The next time you play a board game, remember that the Vikings, more than a thousand years ago, were already challenging each other around a board, honing their strategic skills.

Fact 50 - Goddess Loki: cunning and mischievous.

Loki, often associated with lying and deception in Norse mythology, is a fascinating character. But beware, contrary to what you might think when reading the title, Loki is not really a goddess. In reality, Loki is often described as a god, but his fluid nature makes him unique among Norse deities.

One of the most famous stories about him is the one where he transforms into a mare to seduce a stallion, in order to fool a giant and prevent the construction of a wall around Asgard. From this union will be born Sleipnir, the eight-legged horse of Odin.

Loki possesses this ability to change form and genre at will, making him elusive and enigmatic. His tricks and metamorphoses played tricks on almost all the gods of Asgard, sometimes to help them, other times to deceive them.

So, the next time you hear about Loki, remember that this complex character is not limited to his evil tricks. It is the reflection of a mythology rich in nuances and surprises.

Fact 51 - Distant spices in the kitchen.

Maybe when you think of medieval cuisine, you imagine bland dishes with little variety. Think again! The cuisines of the time were full of exotic spices, often from distant lands.

Since the Middle Ages, thanks to trade routes such as the Silk Road, spices such as pepper, cinnamon, ginger, or saffron have found their way to European tables. These products were so valuable that they were sometimes used as currency, and owning a bag of cloves, for example, was an undeniable sign of wealth.

These spices were not only used for their taste. They were also prized for their medicinal properties. It was believed, for example, that ginger could cure stomach upset and cinnamon could help fight colds.

So the next time you prepare a spicy dish, remember that these exotic flavors have a long and fascinating history, weaving a link between cultures across the ages and continents.

Fact 52 - The Battle of Stamford Bridge.

Did you know that Viking rule in England came to an abrupt end in a decisive battle, before the Normans entered the scene? This battle is that of Stamford Bridge, which took place on September 25, 1066.

The Viking army, led by King Harald Hardrada of Norway, hoped to conquer England. However, they were taken by surprise by the Anglo-Saxon army of King Harold Godwinson, who rushed from southern England to defend his kingdom.

One of the most famous moments of this battle is the fight of a lone Viking warrior, posted on a bridge, who resisted valiantly, single-handedly repelling many English soldiers. Although he was eventually defeated, his courage is still praised today.

Unfortunately for the Vikings, despite their bravery, they were defeated at Stamford Bridge. This defeat marked the end of Viking attempts to conquer England. But for Harold Godwinson, the victory was short-lived, as he soon had to turn his attention to a new threat: the Norman invasion led by William the Conqueror.

Fact 53 - Swords named and cherished.

You've probably heard of famous swords in literature or movies, haven't you? Well, for the Vikings, it wasn't just folklore. They had a fascinating tradition of naming their swords, often reflecting their qualities or the feats they had accomplished.

For a Viking, his sword was much more than just a weapon. It was a symbol of status, honour and bravery. These swords, forged with care, were often passed down from generation to generation, accumulating stories and legends about them.

Names such as "Dragonbite" or "Northern Flame" were not uncommon. These names evoked the power, majesty or supernatural qualities of the sword. Having a named sword was a hallmark of a renowned warrior, and these names were often mentioned in sagas and songs.

Thus, for the Vikings, a sword was not just a tool of war. She was a companion, an integral part of their identity, and a link between past, present and future. Naming his sword was therefore a way of giving him a soul and honoring him.

Fact 54 - Viking tattoos: art and beliefs.

Have you ever thought about getting a Viking tattoo? If so, you're not the only one! For centuries, Viking symbols and motifs have been a source of inspiration. But did you know that the Vikings themselves also wore tattoos?

It is mentioned in some historical sources, such as the writings of the Arab traveler Ibn Fadlan, that the Vikings were tattooed from the fingers to the neck. These tattoos were not mere ornaments. They often reflected Viking beliefs, legends and cosmology.

The exact motives of Viking tattoos are subject to debate among researchers, as very little direct evidence has survived. However, mythical animals, runes and intertwined patterns are thought to have been common. These symbols had a deep meaning, connecting warriors to their gods and ancestors.

So, if you are considering a Viking tattoo, you are not only diving into ancient art, but also into a world of beliefs and traditions that have spanned the ages. A beautiful way to honor a rich and mysterious culture!

Fact 55 - The precious comb of every day.

When you think of the Vikings, you probably imagine savage and boorish warriors. But did you know that the comb was an essential object in their daily lives? Yes, these fearsome navigators were also concerned about their appearance!

Viking combs were often made from bone or horn, and their manufacture required special know-how. Found in many archaeological sites, these combs testify to their importance in Viking society.

Far from being mere tools for styling one's hair, they were also status symbols. A well-worked and ornate comb was a sign of wealth. Some were even accompanied by a small leather or fabric pouch, showing how much they were cherished.

So, the next time you paint yourself, think about the Vikings, their unexpected refinement, and the importance of this small object that, through the centuries, has remained an indispensable part of everyday life.

Fact 56 - The mythical sea serpent.

Have you ever heard of the sea serpent, the mystical creature that haunted the stories of Viking navigators? It wasn't just an invention to scare the young warriors around the campfire. It was deeply rooted in Norse mythology.

The Jörmungandr, as it is called in the sagas, was a gigantic serpent, so large that it could surround the Earth and bite its tail. Son of Loki, this sea serpent was destined to play a major role during Ragnarök, the end of the world according to Viking cosmogony.

Viking sailors, during their expeditions, often reported seeing this terrifying beast emerging from the depths of the ocean. Some saw it as omens, others as a mere coincidence with large fish or giant squid.

From legends to encounters with real, misidentified sea creatures, the sea serpent remains a powerful symbol of the unexplored vastness of the ocean and the mysteries the Vikings sought to unravel.

Fact 57 - Hedeby's bustling market.

Have you ever imagined what a thriving Viking market would look like? Hedeby, located in present-day Germany near the Danish border, was one of the most important trading centers of the Viking Age.

As soon as you walked through the gates of this port city, your senses would have been assailed by a myriad of scents, sounds and colors. Merchants from Scandinavia, Russia, the Middle East and other parts of Europe flocked to Hedeby, displaying their exotic wares: silk, spices, amber, furs, slaves and much more.

Besides goods, Hedeby was also a cultural crossroads. Strolling through the busy streets, you could have heard a mosaic of languages and admired a variety of clothes and art objects, reflecting the different origins of locals and visitors.

Although the archaeological site of Hedeby is now peaceful, it remains a living testimony to the dynamism and diversity of the Vikings, far beyond the image of the barbarian looters that history has often bequeathed to us.

Fact 58 - The art of runes on bone and wood.

Did you know that the Vikings didn't just use stones to engrave messages? Although runestones are famous, bone and wood were also common supports for rune art.

When you discover these objects, they often seem simple, even rudimentary. However, behind each engraved line hides a precise know-how. The runes were not just an alphabet, but also carried a mystical meaning. On bone and wood, the messages were often more personal, sometimes even tinged with humor or magic.

Each engraved object tells a story. A piece of wood can reveal a love poem, a blessing for a newborn or a spell to protect its owner. The bone, often in the form of animal fragments, was used for both incantations and everyday messages.

Today, these artifacts are priceless. They offer an intimate insight into the daily lives, beliefs and emotions of the Vikings, far beyond the great sagas and warrior exploits.

Fact 59 - Drakkars as graves.

Have you ever heard of Viking burials in the shape of boats? Yes, the drakkars, those iconic ships, weren't just made for war or trade. They also had a sacred role in the journey to the afterlife.

Imagine walking through a field and falling on the silhouette of a boat, but with no water around. Not a shipwreck, but a grave. The Vikings firmly believed that their deceased needed transportation for their next journey, whether to Valhalla or other realms in the afterlife.

In these burials, the deceased was not alone. Often he was accompanied by personal items, weapons and sometimes even sacrificed animals or servants, all to ensure a comfortable and honorable passage to the other world.

Today, these drakkar-shaped tombs are poignant testimonies to the depth of Viking beliefs, their love for the sea and their respect for those who left before them.

Fact 60 - The truth about horned helmets.

Ah, the mythical horned helmet! When you think of Vikings, chances are this iconic image will come to mind. But do you know that this representation is actually a myth?

First, there is no archaeological evidence that the Vikings wore horned helmets in battle. In fact, these horns would have been very impractical during battles, as they could have easily hung on or offered a point of capture to the enemy.

So where did this idea come from? It is largely the fruit of the imagination of the 19th century, especially artists and writers who sought to give an exotic and wild look to the Vikings. Plays and operas, such as Richard Wagner's "The Ring of the Nibelung", have largely contributed to anchoring this image in popular culture.

So the next time you see a Viking with a horned helmet in a movie or series, you'll know it's more about show than real story!

Fact 61 - The mystery of the island of Greenland.

You've probably heard of Greenland, that huge icy island west of Iceland. But do you know how it was discovered and named by the Vikings?

Well, it was Erik the Red, a Viking explorer banished from Iceland for murder, who discovered Greenland towards the end of the tenth century. After sailing west, he came across this land, which he decided to call "Greenland" (or "Green Land" in Old Norse).

But why such a name for a mostly icy island? It was actually a marketing stunt! Erik hoped that this attractive name would encourage others to settle there. And it worked! Several Vikings followed in his footsteps, establishing settlements that lasted for about 500 years.

However, these colonies mysteriously disappeared in the fifteenth century. Despite numerous theories, the exact fate of the Viking settlers of Greenland remains a fascinating mystery of history.

Fact 62 - The winter solstice festival.

Do you know the importance of the winter solstice in ancient traditions? For many cultures, including the Vikings, this moment marked a crucial celebration.

For the Norse peoples, this time of year, when the days were shortest and the nights the longest, was an opportunity to celebrate the "Yule" or "Jól" in Old Norse. During this festival, which could last up to twelve days, the Vikings paid homage to the gods, hoping to guarantee the clemency of winter and the fertility of the coming spring.

The festivities were great! Animals were sacrificed in honor of the gods, and their meat was used as a meal for the banquet. They also lit a large bonfire, a symbol of light in the heart of winter darkness, and drank mead in song.

Some Yule rituals persisted and adapted over time. So, if you're decorating a tree during the Christmas season or enjoying a festive meal with your family, know that you're perpetuating, in some way, ancestral traditions related to the winter solstice.

Fact 63 - Circular forts: unique architecture.

Have you ever wondered how the Vikings protected their land? Among their architectural prowess, the circular forts stand out for their ingenuity and robustness.

These fortifications, known as "trelleborgs", were characterized by a perfectly circular shape, with a diameter of up to 150 meters. Surrounded by massive palisades and flanked by watchtowers at regular intervals, these forts were formidable defensive structures.

Inside this enclosure, the buildings were arranged in an orderly manner, often in four symmetrical quarters, each including houses for warriors and their families. The central layout allowed for effective coordination in the event of an attack and also provided space for daily activities and gatherings.

If you have the opportunity to visit Denmark, several of these circular forts are still visible, witnesses of Viking ingenuity in terms of fortifications. These constructions are not only bastions of war, but also vibrant centers of Viking daily life.

Fact 64 - Viking knitting.

Have you ever considered knitting as a Viking activity? Well, know that these northern warriors were not only navigators and fighters; They were also skilled with their hands when it came to textiles.

The Vikings used a technique called "nalbinding". Unlike modern knitting that uses two needles, nalbinding requires only one thick needle, often made from bone or wood. The technique, although complex, made it possible to create dense and warm fabrics, perfect for the harsh climates of the North.

Archaeologists have discovered several artifacts, such as socks, mittens and hats, created with this method. These pieces, in addition to being functional, demonstrate a particular attention to detail and a great mastery of art.

So the next time you're considering knitting a scarf or hat, why not take inspiration from the Vikings? Embrace nalbinding and reconnect with ancient crafts, while keeping warm the Viking way!

Fact 65 - Rare spices in their dishes.

When you imagine Viking cuisine, images of grilled meats and smoked fish may come to mind. However, have you ever considered that these northern warriors also had a taste for rare spices?

In reality, the Vikings were ardent traders and their journeys took them far beyond their northern shores. Through this trade, they had access to exotic spices, such as cumin, coriander, and even cardamom. These spices were valuable commodities, often used to enhance the taste of dishes or to preserve food.

Archaeological finds have unearthed remains of these spices in ancient Viking settlements, testifying to their use in cooking. These spices were not only a luxury; they reflected the wealth and social status of those who could afford them.

So, the next time you enjoy a spicy dish, remember that even the Vikings, with their helmets and swords, had a soft spot for flavor-rich cuisine!

Fact 66 - From Iceland to Newfoundland.

When you think of the Vikings, you may imagine them sailing across the North Seas, but did you know that they had reached lands far beyond Europe? Yes, their sturdy drakkars led them to the New World.

It all started in Iceland. The Vikings had settled there in the ninth century, using the island as a base for their more distant expeditions. Erik the Red, a daring Viking explorer, was the first to colonize Greenland after being banished from Iceland. This new establishment would become a crucial step for subsequent travel.

The real feat came with his son, Leif Erikson. Driven by stories from a land further west, he embarked on a journey that took him to what we know today as Newfoundland, Canada. This was about 500 years before Christopher Columbus "discovered" the New World!

The settlement of L'Anse aux Meadows, an archaeological site in Newfoundland, is concrete proof of this. So, when you think about the great discoveries, remember that the Vikings paved the way long before many others!

Fact 67 - Alliances with distant kings.

The image of the Vikings as ferocious looters is well anchored in the popular mind. But, do you know that they were also skilled diplomats? Indeed, their influence extended far beyond their raids, through strategic alliances with distant kingdoms.

Medieval Russia is a perfect example. The origin of the name "Rus", which gave its name to Russia, is often attributed to the Vikings. They established commercial and political relations with the Slavic peoples, founding cities and integrating the local nobility.

On the other side of Europe, in England, several Vikings not only established colonies, but also made pacts with Anglo-Saxon kings. Some even ascended the throne, such as King Knut the Great who ruled a vast empire including England, Denmark and part of Norway.

These alliances allowed the Vikings to increase their influence, exchange knowledge and enrich themselves. They were much more than mere warriors; They were also diplomats and strategists.

Fact 68 - The place of children in the sagas.

When you dive into the world of Viking sagas, these epic tales of heroes, gods and adventures, have you ever noticed the role that children play? Far from being mere extras, they often occupy a central place in these stories.

Children, symbols of the future and continuity, were essential actors in the family heritage. In the sagas, they may be the holders of prophecies, announcing major events or dynastic changes. Sometimes they embody revenge for an unjustly killed family member, thus continuing intergenerational feuds.

It is also common to see them undertake heroic quests at a young age. These stories show not only their bravery, but also how Viking culture valued early training in combat and strategy.

So the next time you read a Viking saga, pay attention to these young characters. They offer a fascinating perspective on how the Vikings perceived youth, heritage and destiny.

Fact 69 - The key role of women in business.

Have you ever thought about the role of women in business throughout history? Beyond prejudices and clichés, women have often been invisible pillars of the economy.

In the Middle Ages, for example, when society was dominated by men, women played a crucial role in family affairs. In the absence of their husbands, they often managed shops, workshops and took care of finances. They were also skilled negotiators, forging business alliances and closing deals.

In some cultures, women's talent for business was particularly recognized. In the Italian city-states of the Renaissance, for example, women dominated the ready-to-set market, a lucrative industry of the time.

Thus, long before they were legally and socially recognized, women have always been essential actors on the economic scene. Their contribution, though often underestimated, has shaped the history of business far more than we think.

Fact 70 - The Jomsviking: elite warriors.

Have you ever heard of the Jomsvikings? These Scandinavian warriors, active between the tenth and eleventh centuries, were reputed to be the elite among the Vikings.

Hailing from Jomsborg, a legendary fortress on the southern coast of the Baltic Sea, these fighters followed a strict code of conduct. To be admitted to their ranks, one had to prove one's worth in battle and swear to abide by their laws, which forbade fear and lies.

These warriors were not only exceptional fighters, but also wanted mercenaries. Their loyalty was only bought at a high price, and they were known to never break a contract, regardless of the opponent or obstacles.

As you delve into Norse history, you'll discover that the Jomsvikings, with their iron discipline and bravery in battle, left their mark on the sagas and epic tales of the time. Further proof of the richness and complexity of Viking history.

Fact 71 - The creation of the world according to them.

Have you ever explored Viking beliefs about the creation of the world? Their vision is as fascinating as it is unique.

In the beginning, there was only emptiness, an abyss named Ginnungagap, surrounded by two opposite worlds: Muspell, the burning world, and Niflheim, the cold world. When these two worlds met, the interaction between fire and ice gave birth to the giant Ymir and the primordial cow, Audhumla.

From these primordial beings, everything began to take shape. Feeding on Audhumla's milk, Ymir gave birth to other giants. Moreover, by licking the salt ice, Audhumla revealed the first god: Buri. Buri's descendants, Odin and his brothers, eventually killed Ymir, using his body to create the world as we know it: his blood forming the oceans, his bones the mountains, and his head the sky.

Through this captivating myth, you can glimpse how the Vikings perceived life, death and the eternal cycle of creation. A vision quite distinct from other mythologies of the world.

Fact 72 - The mysterious island named Vinland.

Have you heard of Vinland? This distant land, evoked in the Viking sagas, represents one of the greatest mysteries of medieval navigation.

Vinland is described in the Icelandic sagas as a rich land, located west of Greenland. The descriptions speak of lush territories, with meadows as far as the eye can see and trees large enough to build ships. Leif Erikson, son of Erik the Red, is generally credited with his discovery in the early 11th century.

Archaeological evidence shows that the Vikings did indeed reach North America, long before Christopher Columbus. At L'Anse aux Meadows, Newfoundland, Canada, remnants of Viking encampments have been discovered, suggesting they may have explored further south.

Could Vinland be part of present-day North America? The question remains open. But one thing is certain: the Vikings were true pioneers, braving the unknown and expanding the horizons of the known world.

Fact 73 - The first map of the Viking world.

Have you ever wondered how the Vikings, those intrepid navigators, orient themselves during their travels? The answer may well surprise you.

The Vikings did not use sophisticated compasses or modern navigational instruments. Instead, they had sagas, songs, and in some cases, maps. One of the most famous is the map of Skálholt. Dating back to the 16th century, it is based on older sources and shows the Viking worldview.

This map shows Europe, Asia, Greenland, and a mysterious land called "Vinland" - probably part of North America. The distances are not exact, and the orientation is different from current standards, but it shows a deep curiosity and thirst for discovery.

Imagine sailing the turbulent seas with this map as your only guide. The Vikings didn't just explore; They mapped and shared their knowledge, establishing the first transatlantic routes.

Fact 74 - The forgotten fortress of Danevirke.

Have you ever heard of Danevirke? No? This is hardly surprising, because despite its historical importance, it is often overshadowed by other Viking achievements.

Located in present-day northern Germany, Danevirke is a series of fortifications stretching over 30 kilometers. Erected from the 6th century, it served as a defensive barrier for the Danish kingdom, protecting the land from invaders from the south.

Over the centuries, the fortress has been strengthened and expanded several times. The walls, lined with deep ditches, were a feat of engineering for the time. Despite its strategic importance, Danevirke eventually fell into disuse, as borders and military needs evolved.

Today, if you go there, you will still be able to see the traces of this gigantic fortification, testifying to the genius and determination of the Vikings to protect their territories. A forgotten but essential page in the history of the North.

Fact 75 - Sacred respect for nature.

Do you know how much the Vikings revered nature? For them, each natural element had its own energy, its own aura, constantly interacting with man.

Forests, mountains and rivers were not just resources or obstacles. They were populated by spirits, elves and mythical creatures. Cutting down a tree or navigating a river required respect and precaution. Offending these entities could lead to misfortune and disaster.

Nature was also a source of guidance. The Vikings carefully observed star movements, animal behavior, and climate change to make decisions, whether for navigation or agriculture.

So next time you walk in nature, try to see the world through the eyes of a Viking. Feel the presence of every tree, every stone, and remember how essential it is to treat our environment with respect and gratitude.

Fact 76 - The legend of the berserkers.

Have you ever heard of the fearsome Viking berserkers? These warriors were famous for their rage in battle, entering frenzied trances that gave them superhuman strength and resistance.

The word "berserker" probably comes from the Old Norse "ber-serkr", meaning "bear's shirt". Some believe that these warriors wore bear skins during battles, while others suggest that they literally turned into bears during their trances. Legends also associate them with wolves, sometimes calling them "ulfhednar" or "wolf-men".

Some say that these trances were induced by shamanic rituals, drugs, or were the result of spiritual gifts. These states allowed the berserkers not to feel pain and terrify their enemies with their ferocity.

So, the next time you hear the word "berserk", remember the Viking warriors, their legendary rage and the mystery that still surrounds the true nature of their trances today.

Fact 77 - Write history with runes.

Have you ever seen these mysterious symbols engraved on Viking stones or jewelry? These are runes, the writing system of the Germanic peoples long before the introduction of the Latin alphabet.

The runes were not just letters, they were also loaded with esoteric meanings. Each rune had a name and represented a concept or object, such as "fehu" for cattle or wealth, and "uruz" for auroch or strength. This double meaning made it a powerful tool for magic and rituals.

The runestones, often erected as memorials, are precious witnesses of Viking history. They tell stories of heroes, distant journeys or exploits in war. Some messages are poetic, others practical, but all offer a unique insight into their time.

The next time you come across a rune, know that it is much more than just a symbol. It is a window into the past, a link to an ancient culture and a rich history written in mystical letters.

Fact 78 - The real treasure: talented slaves.

Have you ever heard of Viking looting? True, gold and silver were coveted treasures, but there was another "resource" just as precious to them: talented slaves.

Contrary to popular belief, not all slaves were treated equally. Those with specific skills, such as crafts, music, or medicine, were particularly prized. These slaves, called "thralls", could sometimes enjoy a better quality of life, depending on their talents and their master.

The slave trade was a lucrative business for the Vikings, and they often sold these talented individuals at high prices in distant markets, such as Constantinople or Andalusia. The expertise of a slave could therefore give him a certain value and allow him to escape a life of intense labor.

Reflecting on this, it is fascinating to think that, despite the stereotypes of brutal barbarians, the Vikings recognized and valued skills and talent, even in those they had enslaved.

Fact 79 - Rival peoples and friends.

Did you know that the Vikings, despite their reputation as fierce warriors, also had allies and trade relations with many cultures? Accounts of looting have often obscured this more peaceful dimension of their history.

Beyond their famous raids, the Vikings established colonies and engaged in trade with peoples such as the Arabs, Byzantines, and Slavs. They imported products such as silk, spices or jewellery, while exporting northern goods such as amber, fur or iron.

It is true that they had conflicts with certain peoples, such as the Anglo-Saxons or the Franks, but they also forged alliances, especially through marriages. Viking princesses were sometimes married to foreign kings to seal peace pacts.

So the next time you hear about the Vikings, remember that they were not only warriors, but also traders, explorers and diplomats, forging bonds of friendship and rivalry around the world.

Fact 80 - The great Viking markets.

When you think of the Vikings, you might imagine warriors wielding their swords. But did you know that they were also skilled traders, having established flourishing markets?

At the time, Viking markets, such as Birka in Sweden or Hedeby in Denmark, were important trading centers. They attracted merchants from various backgrounds, eager to exchange goods from distant lands. Imagine a lively bazaar, where the echoes of the negotiations mingle with the laughter and shouts of the sellers.

The goods traded varied greatly. Silver jewelry from the Orient, colorful textiles from Southern Europe, and of course, local products like amber, dried fish or furs. These markets were crossroads of cultures, places where traditions and ideas intersected.

Thus, far from being just looters, the Vikings played a major role in the trade of the time. These markets demonstrate their ability to establish trade networks and integrate diverse cultures into a single civilization.

Fact 81 - The transition from paganism to Christianity.

When you delve into the history of the Vikings, you discover a fascinating spiritual journey. Did you know that these warriors and explorers, initially pagans, gradually converted to Christianity?

In the beginning, the Vikings worshipped multiple gods, such as Odin, Thor or Freyja. Their beliefs were deeply rooted in nature and the elements. Trees, stones and springs were considered sacred. They celebrated rituals and festivals that marked the seasons and important events in life.

However, from the 10th century, the winds of change blew. Through travel and exchange with other cultures, especially in England and France, the Vikings were exposed to Christianity. Viking kings and chieftains, seeing the political and economic benefits of Christianity, began to embrace this new faith, sometimes by force, encouraging their subjects to do the same.

By the end of the 11th century, Scandinavia had become predominantly Christian. But this transition has not completely erased old beliefs. Many pagan elements have been integrated and adapted, leaving a lasting imprint on Scandinavian culture.

Fact 82 - Jewelry to seduce and show its wealth.

Let's immerse ourselves in the brilliance of Viking jewels, you will be fascinated. For them, jewelry was much more than just ornaments. They were symbols of status, power and charm.

In the Viking Age, gold, silver and bronze were worked with remarkable skill. Artisans created exquisite bracelets, necklaces, brooches and rings. These pieces were often decorated with intertwined motifs, mythical animals and precious stones. Every detail reflected the talent and creativity of its creator.

These jewels were not just fashion accessories. They were also used as bargaining chips during transactions. The more jewelry a Viking owned, the more influential and wealthy he was considered to be. Jewelry was therefore both an investment and an outward sign of wealth.

In addition, in the context of seduction, offering a jewel was a strong gesture. It was a show of affection, but also a way to attract and charm. Viking jewelry was thus at the heart of the social, economic and romantic relations of this society.

Fact 83 - The first parliaments in Iceland.

Iceland, this wild territory of the North, will surprise you with its pioneering role in democracy. Indeed, it housed one of the very first parliaments in the world, the famous Althing.

Founded in 930 AD, the Althing was not just a gathering of leaders. It was an annual open-air meeting where clan chiefs met to discuss laws, settle disputes, and make decisions concerning the entire island. The chosen location, Thingvellir, had both geological and symbolic significance, lying between the tectonic plates of North America and Eurasia.

One of the most fascinating aspects of this assembly was its "Lögsögumaður", or "Man of Law". He recited aloud all the laws to make sure everyone knew about them. No written text was used, everything was based on memory.

This gathering, which combined justice, legislation and sociability, foreshadowed modern democracies. It shows that long before the introduction of the parliamentary system in Europe, Iceland had already laid the foundations for collective and participatory governance.

Fact 84 - The gods of animals: wolf, raven...

Have you ever heard of the deep relationship between Vikings and animals in their mythology? These creatures play major roles, reflecting strong values and symbols in the lives of these northern peoples.

Wolves, for example, have a fascinating duality. Fenrir, the gigantic wolf, is one of Loki's children and is destined to play a devastating role in Ragnarök, the end of the world. Yet other wolves, such as Geri and Freki, are the faithful companions of the god Odin, reflecting both savagery and loyalty.

Crows also have a special place. Huginn (thought) and Muninn (memory) are Odin's two ravens. Every day, they travel the world to gather information and report it to their master. These birds symbolize Odin's insatiable quest to find out.

Overall, every animal in Viking mythology carries a meaning and essence that transcends its physical form. They reflect the complexity of nature, gods and men, and their interconnected relationships.

Fact 85 - Feasts in honor of the gods.

Do you know how much the Vikings wanted to honor their gods? Feasts were one of the grandest ways to show their devotion, mixing abundance and sacred rituals.

First, these ceremonies were not mere meals. They were carefully prepared, often for several days, with animals specially bred for the occasion. These feasts were an opportunity for the community to come together, thus strengthening social and religious ties.

Beverages, especially mead, had a central place. Served in horns or intricately decorated goblets, they were shared in honor of gods like Odin or Freyja. Toasts were made, not only to the gods but also in memory of the ancestors who had disappeared.

Finally, these feasts were not only gastronomic. They were accompanied by songs, epic tales and prayers. These moments were a bridge between men and the divine, a way for the Vikings to thank, honor and solicit the benevolence of their gods.

Fact 86 - The mysterious red woman of Oseberg.

Have you ever heard of the red woman of Oseberg? This mysterious figure is at the heart of one of the most fascinating and enigmatic Viking archaeological finds.

In 1904, in Norway, Oseberg's tomb was discovered. It contained a majestic Viking ship, as well as the remains of two women. One of them, because of traces of red pigments found on her teeth, was nicknamed "the red woman". This pigment would come from a regular consumption of dyed textiles, an enigma in itself.

Speculation abounds about the identity of this woman. Was she a priestess, queen, shaman, or perhaps a high-ranking embroiderer? His presence in such a sumptuous tomb undoubtedly indicates a high status.

Oseberg's tomb has left us with many treasures and artifacts, but it is this mysterious red woman that continues to captivate and intrigue researchers and history buffs. Who was she really? Her mystery remains, making her an icon of the Viking Age.

Fact 87 - How to educate a young Viking.

Have you ever wondered how a young Viking was educated in the golden age of their explorations? Viking education was very different from what we know today, focused on survival, courage and tradition.

From an early age, boys were introduced to hunting and fishing, vital skills for their survival in the often hostile environments of Scandinavia. The stories of their ancestors, the sagas, were told to them, reinforcing their cultural identity and teaching them Viking values.

The girls, meanwhile, learned their mothers' domestic skills: weaving, cooking, and managing the home. But be careful, this does not mean that they were less valuable. Some Viking women were also trained in combat, proving their strength just as much as men.

Viking education was not only practical, it was deeply rooted in their culture and beliefs, preparing the younger generation to face life's challenges while honoring gods and ancestors.

Fact 88 - Dancing and singing in the light of fire.

Have you ever imagined a Viking evening around a crackling fire, where music and dancing were the main attractions? Fire was at the heart of the Vikings' social life, and their nightly festivities were much more than just entertainment.

These evenings were often an opportunity for the community to come together. As the flames danced, musicians played melodies on lyres and drums, creating a haunting atmosphere. These instruments, simple but effective, were the pillars of Viking music.

Dancing, on the other hand, wasn't just entertainment. It was used to tell stories, celebrate events, or even honor the gods. The movements were energetic, reflecting the vitality and strength of the Viking people.

Beyond mere joy, these moments around the fire were a way for the Vikings to connect with each other, with their traditions and beliefs. They reminded everyone of the importance of community and the joy of living every moment to the fullest.

Fact 89 - The mystical sun compass.

Have you ever wondered how the Vikings, those famous navigators, headed on their vast expeditions? One of their secrets was the solar compass, a fascinating and mystical invention.

Consisting of a stone disc with a rod in its center, this compass exploited shadows to determine the position of the sun, even on cloudy days. They often used a special crystal, the sunstone, to detect the sun through clouds, enhancing the accuracy of their navigation.

But this compass was not only a practical instrument; It was also surrounded by symbolism. The circle represented the universe, while the central rod symbolized the axis around which the world revolves. The Vikings saw a connection between nature, cosmology and their daily lives.

Thus, thanks to the solar compass, the Vikings not only traced their way through the raging seas, but they also moved closer to understanding the cosmos, skillfully blending science and spirituality.

Fact 90 - The sagas: stories of heroes and gods.

Have you ever heard of the Viking sagas? These epic tales tell of the exploits of heroes, the intrigues of the gods and the destinies of kings. It is thanks to these sagas that we know so many details about the culture and history of the Vikings.

Written in Old Norse, these stories were often recited at large gatherings or around the fire, passing on wisdom, honour and traditions from generation to generation. They served not only as entertainment, but also as education for young people.

The sagas were not simply fictional stories. Many were based on real events and historical figures, offering valuable insight into Viking life, their conflicts, loves, betrayals and discoveries. Sagas such as that of Egill Skallagrímsson or the Saga of the Ynglingar bring this distant period to life.

So, if you want to dive into the world of the Vikings, there's nothing like immersing yourself in their sagas. These stories will transport you to a world where the gods walked alongside men, and where honor was worth more than gold.

Fact 91 - The secret role of volvas (prophetesses).

Do you remember the tales where mystical figures, draped in capes, predict the future with disconcerting precision? In Viking society, these figures were known as "volvas". These prophetesses played an essential, often unrecognized, role in their community.

Richly dressed, wearing rings and ornate sticks, these women were respected and feared. Their ability to communicate with the gods, predict the future, and influence destiny made them sought-after advisors by kings and warlords. Imagine the power of a voice that can predict the outcome of a battle or the next great harvest!

But they weren't just reading the future. They were also healers, using herbs and rituals to heal and protect their people. Their wisdom in matters of plants and spirits was unmatched.

So the next time you think of the Vikings, don't forget those powerful women, whose voices and visions influenced the destinies of strong men and entire nations.

Fact 92 - Raising eagles to hunt.

Have you ever imagined hunting not with a dog, but with a majestic eagle? This is exactly what some peoples have been doing since ancient times. Raising eagles for hunting is an ancient art, known as falconry, although the term can be confusing.

These eagles, called hunting eagles, were trained from an early age to become formidable predators. With a wingspan of up to more than 2 meters for some species, they were able to spot and catch prey ranging from hares to foxes. Imagine the necessary complicity between man and bird to achieve such a feat!

The training of these eagles required considerable patience and expertise. Each eagle had to be fed, trained and cared for with absolute dedication, thus strengthening the special bond between the bird and its master.

So, the next time you see an eagle hovering high in the sky, remember that it could be the heir of a thousand-year-old tradition, a symbol of the symbiosis between man and nature.

Fact 93 - Sailing with wind and currents.

Have you ever wondered how, before the invention of modern navigational instruments, sailors sailed on the vast oceans? The secret lies in their ability to understand wind and currents.

Since ancient times, navigators have learned to "read" the sea. By observing the movements of the water and the variations of the wind, they could determine the direction to take. It was not just a simple intuition, but a science based on observation and experience accumulated over generations.

Sea currents, these natural highways, were used to speed up the journey. Sailors were particularly attentive to changes in water temperature and salinity, signs of the presence of a current. Similarly, by observing the behavior of birds and fish, they could deduce the direction of favorable winds and currents.

So, the next time you look at the sea, think of those daring navigators who, armed with their knowledge and intuition, braved the oceans by relying on the natural elements.

Fact 94 - The rite of passage of the young warrior.

Have you ever heard of the rites of passage that young warriors had to undergo in certain cultures? These ceremonies were much more than just traditions, they marked the transition from childhood to adulthood.

In many ancient societies, a young man was not simply considered a warrior because of his age. He had to prove his bravery, strength and determination. These trials could vary from culture to culture, ranging from hunting a dangerous animal, to surviving alone in the wild for several days.

These rites were not just a demonstration of physical strength. They were also a mental test, where the young person had to show his ability to endure pain, loneliness and fear. It was a way to ensure that only the most deserving would achieve the coveted warrior status.

So the next time you hear about rites of passage, remember that they reflected the values and ideals of an entire society, shaping the warriors of tomorrow.

Fact 95 - The Faroese: Vikings of the islands.

Have you ever heard of the Faroe Islands, this small archipelago lost in the North Atlantic? This is where the Faroese lived, direct descendants of the Vikings and undisputed masters of the sea.

The first settlers of the Faroe Islands were Irish monks, but they were soon followed by Norwegian Vikings in the ninth century. These seasoned navigators were looking for new land to settle. These islands, although beaten by the winds, offered fertile land and seas rich in fish.

Living in this isolated environment, Faroese developed a unique culture, while retaining many of the Viking traditions. For example, "Ólavsøka", a Faroese national holiday, is actually a celebration in honor of King Olaf II of Norway, a legacy of their former allegiance to the Norwegian crown.

Thus, even if the Faroe Islands may seem remote and isolated, they are the living testimony of a Viking culture that has been able to adapt and endure through the ages. If you have the opportunity to visit them, you will certainly feel the echo of the songs and sagas of yesteryear.

Fact 96 - Teeth engraved to impress.

You've probably seen tattoos or body scarifications used as ornaments or symbols of identity. But have you ever heard of the Vikings engraving their teeth? It was both an aesthetic and intimidating practice.

In the tenth century, archaeologists discovered Viking skeletons with horizontal streaks carved on their upper incisors. The precise reason for this bodily modification remains a mystery, but it is likely that it had a social or warlike significance.

Some believe that these dental engravings were a way for warriors to show their bravery, resistance to pain, or perhaps belonging to a specific group. Others suggest that they were simply aesthetic, much like our modern piercings or tattoos.

Either way, one thing is certain: these distinctive marks were probably a reflection of a deep desire to impress, whether by seducing or intimidating the enemy. Can you imagine the reaction of seeing a Viking warrior smiling with teeth engraved before the fight? A certainly impressive vision!

Fact 97 - Laws written on wood.

At a time when paper was scarce and expensive, the Vikings came up with an ingenious solution. You've heard of engraved runes before, haven't you? But did you know that the Vikings also wrote their laws on pieces of wood?

These sticks, called "sticks of law", were used by Viking rulers to transcribe and propagate rules and judicial decisions. Engraving on wood allowed for impressive durability, indispensable in a humid and cold climate.

This process also reflects the importance of oral memory in Viking society. These sticks were often used as memorization aids. At rallies, the "loispeakers" (reciters of the law) read and interpreted these laws for the people.

By engraving the laws on wood, the Vikings demonstrated their pragmatism and respect for the durability of the rules. A beautiful proof of their ability to adapt their way of life to the materials and resources at their disposal. Who would have thought that wood could be the precursor of our current law books?

Fact 98 - Honoring a king with a ship-grave.

Imagine, a large ship, majestic, stranded not on a beach, but in the middle of a green hill. This amazing sight is a tomb ship, and it was the Vikings' way of honoring their kings and great warriors.

The Vikings had a deep relationship with the sea. Their existence depended on travel, conquests and explorations by boat. So, when a Viking leader died, what could be more respectful than offering him a last symbolic journey?

These graves were not just ships. They were filled with treasures, weapons, and sometimes sacrificed animals or servants, so that the deceased would have everything he needed for his journey into the afterlife. These rich tombs are real windows on Viking daily life.

By discovering these tomb boats, archaeologists were able to understand the grandeur and richness of the Vikings. For them, death was a departure, an ultimate journey, and they prepared for it with all the pomp that their status demanded. A beautiful testament to their greatness and their faith.

Fact 99 - The Vikings in Russia: elite merchants.

Have you ever wondered where the name "Russia" comes from? It turns out it's related to the Vikings. Yes, these northern warriors were not only looters, but also shrewd traders, and their travels took them to the lands of present-day Russia.

The first Viking presence in Russia is attested in the 8th century. Known as Varangians, these Vikings ventured along major Russian rivers such as the Volga or the Dnieper. Their goal? Find new trade routes, especially to Byzantium and the Orient, and trade furs, honey and slaves.

The Varangians did not just trade. They established principalities and played a vital role in founding some of Russia's oldest urban centers, including Kiev and Novgorod. Thanks to their maritime and commercial expertise, they quickly gained influence.

So, when you think of the Vikings, remember that they were much more than just warriors. In Russia, they left an indelible mark, not only as conquerors, but above all as builders of civilizations and outstanding merchants.

Fact 100 - Iceland's last Viking chieftain.

Have you ever heard of Snorri Sturluson? He was much more than just a Viking chief. In fact, he was one of the most emblematic figures of medieval Iceland, both as a politician, historian and poet.

Born in 1179, Snorri played a crucial role in Icelandic political affairs. At a time when Iceland was a chessboard for the Norwegian powers, he skillfully maneuvered between rival clans, always seeking to preserve the independence of his native island.

But that's not all. Snorri is best known for his literary contributions. He is the author of the "Prose Edda", a compilation of Norse myths and skaldic poetry. Thanks to him, we now have valuable knowledge of Norse mythology and the art of Viking poetry.

Unfortunately, his political intrigues eventually led to his downfall. In 1241, at the age of 62, Snorri was betrayed and murdered on the orders of the King of Norway. But his legend lives on, and through his writings, Iceland's last great Viking chief lives on.

Conclusion

At the end of this journey through the ages, one thing remains undeniable: the Vikings, far from being mere bloodthirsty barbarians, were a complex people, endowed with a rich cultural, spiritual and social tapestry. Their exploits at sea, their quests for territory and their thirst for knowledge have propelled them to the four corners of Europe and beyond, leaving behind indelible traces.

The 100 facts we explored are just the tip of the iceberg of Viking heritage. Every fact, every story, every legend highlights a unique aspect of their civilization and reminds us how much they helped shape the world we know today.

Dear reader, as you close this book, I hope you will take with you not only increased knowledge about the Vikings, but also an appreciation for their ingenuity, bravery, and indomitable spirit. May their story continue to inspire and amaze future generations, just as it captivated us. And perhaps, at the bend of a calm sea or a dense forest, you will feel the distant echo of Viking songs, reminding you of their immortal exploits.

Marc Dresgui

Quiz

1) **What mystical instrument did the Vikings use to navigate?**

    a) The Lunar Compass
    b) The solar compass
    c) The North Star
    d) The wind compass

2) **Which of the following animals was NOT associated with a Viking god?**

    a) Wolf
    b) Crow
    c) Eagle
    d) Snake

3) **What dental practice did the Vikings use to impress their opponents?**

    a) Teeth whitening
    b) The installation of precious stones
    c) Engraving teeth
    d) Tooth removal

4) **How did the Vikings honor a deceased king?**

    a) By burning it on a pyre
    b) With a tomb boat

c) By burying him with his weapons
d) By mummifying it

5) Which people are known as the "Vikings of the Islands"?

   a) Greenlanders
   b) Norwegians
   c) The Danes
   d) The Faroese

6) Which mystical group of women played an essential role in Viking society?

   a) The Valkyries
   b) The Volvas
   c) The Norns
   d) The Shieldmaidens

7) On what material did the Vikings often write their laws?

   a) On stone
   b) On parchment
   c) On wood
   d) On skin

8) What symbol is associated with the religious transition of the Vikings?

   a) The Solar Cross
   b) Thor's Hammer
   c) The Christian Cross
   d) The wheel of the sun

9) In which region were the Vikings recognized as elite merchants?

   a) In China
   b) In Russia
   c) In Morocco
   d) In India

10) What were the Viking warriors in combat trance called?

   a) Skalds
   b) Huscarls
   c) Berserkers
   d) Ulfhednar

11) Where were the first parliaments held in the Viking Age?

   a) Norway
   b) Denmark

c) Iceland
d) Sweden

12) For what kind of festivity were the Vikings known?

a) Harvest celebrations
b) Feasts in honor of the gods
c) Moon festivals
d) Music festivals

13) What communication tool did the Vikings use to write history?

a) Hieroglyphics
b) Runes
c) Latin scripts
d) Celtic symbols

14) Who was the mysterious woman buried in Oseberg?

a) A queen
b) A warrior
c) A slave
d) A prophetess

15) **In what activities did the Vikings engage in the light of fire?**
   a) Meditation
   b) Dancing and singing
   c) Preparation of potions
   d) Stone cutting

16) **How was a young Viking educated to become a warrior?**
   a) Through showdowns
   b) Hunting with eagles
   c) Via a specific rite of passage
   d) By studying ancient manuscripts

17) **What was the real treasure sought by some Vikings during their raids?**
   a) Gold
   b) Fertile land
   c) Talented slaves
   d) Jewellery

18) **What accessory did the Vikings use to show their wealth?**
   a) Elaborate hairstyles
   b) Jewellery

c) Ornate tattoos
d) Embroidered garments

19) With whom did the Vikings have both friendly and conflictual relations?

   a) The Mongols
   b) The Romans
   c) The Saxons
   d) The Byzantines

20) Who was Iceland's last Viking chieftain?

   a) Harald Hardrada
   b) Leif Erikson
   c) Snorri Sturluson
   d) Ragnald Lothbrok

Answers

1) **What mystical instrument did the Vikings use to navigate?**

   Correct answer: b)The solar compass

2) **Which of the following animals was NOT associated with a Viking god?**

   Correct answer: c)Eagle

3) **What dental practice did the Vikings use to impress their opponents?**

   Correct answer: c)Engrave teeth

4) **How did the Vikings honor a deceased king?**

   Correct answer: b)With a grave boat

5) **Which people are known as the "Vikings of the Islands"?**

   Correct answer: (d)Faroese

6) Which mystical group of women played an essential role in Viking society?

Correct answer: b)The Volvas

7) On what material did the Vikings often write their laws?

Correct answer: c)On wood

8) What symbol is associated with the religious transition of the Vikings?

Correct answer: c) The Christian cross

9) In which region were the Vikings recognized as elite merchants?

Correct answer: b)In Russia

10) What were the Viking warriors in combat trance called?

Correct answer: c)Berserkers

11) **Where were the first parliaments held in the Viking Age?**

Correct answer: c) Iceland

12) **For what kind of festivity were the Vikings known?**

Correct answer: b) Feasts in honor of the gods

13) **What communication tool did the Vikings use to write history?**

Correct answer: b) Runes

14) **Who was the mysterious woman buried in Oseberg?**

Correct answer: d) A prophetess

15) **In what activities did the Vikings engage in the light of fire?**

Correct answer: b) Dancing and singing

16) How was a young Viking educated to become a warrior?

Correct answer: c) Via a specific rite of passage

17) What was the real treasure sought by some Vikings during their raids?

Correct answer: c) Talented slaves

18) What accessory did the Vikings use to show their wealth?

Correct answer: b) Jewelry

19) With whom did the Vikings have both friendly and conflictual relations?

Correct answer: c) The Saxons

20) Who was Iceland's last Viking chieftain?

Correct answer: c) Snorri Sturluson

Printed in Great Britain
by Amazon